W9-AQC-678

Date: 1/19/16

BR 796.334 LIN
Lindeen, Mary.
Let's play soccer! /

A Beginning-to-Read Book

Let's Play Soccer

by Mary Lindeen

NORWOOD HOUSE PRESS

DEAR CAREGIVER, The *Beginning to Read—Read and Discover* books provide emergent readers the opportunity to explore the world through nonfiction while building early reading skills. The text integrates both common sight words and content vocabulary. These key words are featured on lists provided at the back of the book to help your child expand his or her sight word recognition, which helps build reading fluency. The content words expand vocabulary and support comprehension.

Nonfiction text is any text that is factual. The Common Core State Standards call for an increase in the amount of informational text reading among students. The Standards aim to promote college and career readiness among students. Preparation for college and career endeavors requires proficiency in reading complex informational texts in a variety of content areas. You can help your child build a foundation by introducing nonfiction early. To further support the CCSS, you will find Reading Reinforcement activities at the back of the book that are aligned to these Standards.

Above all, the most important part of the reading experience is to have fun and enjoy it!

Sincerely,

Shannon Cannon

Shannon Cannon, Ph.D.
Literacy Consultant

Norwood House Press • P.O. Box 316598 • Chicago, Illinois 60631
For more information about Norwood House Press please visit our website at
www.norwoodhousepress.com or call 866-565-2900.
© 2016 Norwood House Press. Beginning-to-Read™ is a trademark of Norwood House Press.
All rights reserved. No part of this book may be reproduced or utilized in any form or by any
means without written permission from the publisher.

Editor: Judy Kentor Schmauss
Designer: Lindaanne Donohoe

Photo Credits:

Shutterstock, cover, 3 (Natursports), 4-5, 6-7 (Celso Pupo), 18 (Ververidis Vasilis), 9,
14, 15, 18-19 (Jeffersaon Bernardes), 20-21 (Herbert Kratky), 22-23 (mooinblack),
24-25, 26-27 (mooinblack), 28-29 (AGIF); Dreamstime, 1 (©Sswartz), 10-11
(©Luis Lopes Silva), 12-13 (©Stef22), 16-17 (©Stef22)

Library of Congress Cataloging-in-Publication Data
   Lindeen, Mary.
    Lets play soccer / by Mary Lindeen.
      pages cm. – (A Beginning to Read Book)
    Summary: "Soccer is a team sport that is played on a soccer field. Players
wear uniforms and cleats. They run and kick the ball to get it into the
other team's net. Find out about goalies, referees, and how to score points.
This title includes reading activities and a word list"– Provided by publisher.
    Audience: K to Grade 3.
    ISBN 978-1-59953-683-5 (Library Edition : alk. paper)
    ISBN 978-1-60357-768-7 (eBook)
    1. Soccer–Juvenile literature. I. Title. II. Title: Let us play soccer
    GV943.25.L55 2015
    796.334–dc23
                    2014047617

Manufactured in the United States of America in Stevens Point, Wisconsin. 275N-062015

Soccer is a team sport.

People all around the world play soccer.

The game is played on a field.

You use a soccer ball.

Two teams play at a time.

Each team can have 11 players on the field.

The players wear uniforms.
They wear shin guards, too.

Cleats help them run on the grass.

This player is the goalie.

She tries to keep the ball out of the net.

Soccer has referees.

The referees make players follow the rules.

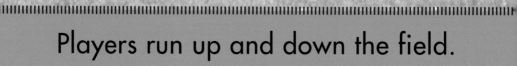

Players run up and down the field.

They kick the ball with their feet.

They hit the ball with their legs or knees.

They even hit
the ball with
their heads!

They must get the
ball into the other
team's net.

Score!

Soccer players can not use their hands.

Only goalies can do that.

Each team wants to get the most points.

Each goal is worth one point.

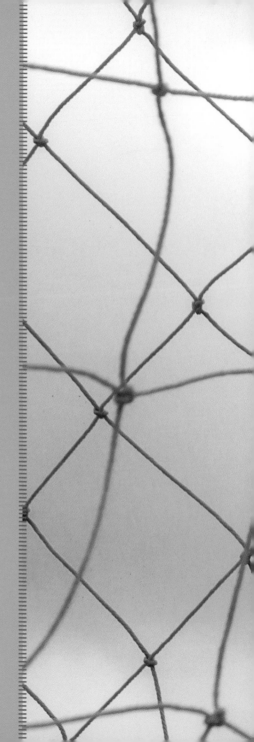

This is the
scoreboard.

It shows how
many points
each team has.

Who is winning?

The game is over.

Everyone did their best.

Good work!

...READING REINFORCEMENT...

CRAFT AND STRUCTURE

To check your child's understanding of this book, recreate the following diagram on a sheet of paper. Read the book with your child, then help him or her fill in the diagram using what they learned. Work together to complete the chart by stating what he or she already knows about soccer, what he or she wants to know, and what he or she learned from reading the book:

What I Know

What I Want to Know

What I Learned

VOCABULARY: Learning Content Words

Content words are words that are specific to a particular topic. All of the content words for this book can be found on page 32. Use some or all of these content words to complete one or more of the following activities:

- Provide clues about the meaning of a content word, and have your child guess the word.

- Make up a story together using as many of the content words as you can.

- Help your child make associations between two content words. Pick any two content words, and have your child think of something these words have in common.

- Create a word web for one or more of the content words. Write the word itself in the center of the web, and synonyms (words with similar meanings), antonyms (words with opposite meanings), or other related words in the outer spokes.

- Ask your child questions that include one or more of the content words. Each question should begin with one of these words: *who*, *what*, *when*, *where*, *why*, or *how*.

FOUNDATIONAL SKILLS: Double consonants

Double consonants are two identical consonants next to each other in a word. The two letters make a single sound. Have your child identify words with double consonants in the list below. Then work with your child to find words with double consonants in this book.

ball/best	soccer/shin	keep/knees
hands/head	winning/worth	field/follow
goal/grass	sport/score	goalie/guards

CLOSE READING OF INFORMATIONAL TEXT

Close reading helps children comprehend text. It includes reading a text, discussing it with others, and answering questions about it. Use these questions to discuss this book with your child:

• How many players are on a soccer field at one time?

• What is the difference between cleats and sneakers?

• How could you use your hands in soccer?

• Why does a soccer game need referees?

• What would happen if a game didn't have referees?

• What is your opinion of soccer?

FLUENCY

Fluency is the ability to read accurately with speed and expression. Help your child practice fluency by using one or more of the following activities:

• Reread this book to your child at least two times while he or she uses a finger to track each word as you read it.

• Read the first sentence aloud. Then have your child reread the sentence with you. Continue until you have finished this book.

• Ask your child to read aloud the words they know on each page of this book. (Your child will learn additional words with subsequent readings.)

• Have your child practice reading this book several times to improve accuracy, rate, and expression.

··· Word List ···

Let's Play Soccer uses the 90 words listed below. *High-frequency* words are those words that are used most often in the English language. They are sometimes referred to as sight words because children need to learn to recognize them automatically when they read. *Content words* are any words specific to a particular topic. Regular practice reading these words will enhance your child's ability to read with greater fluency and comprehension.

High-Frequency Words

a	get	most	people	too
all	good	must	she	two
and	has	not	show(s)	up
around	have	of	that	use
at	help	on	the	want(s)
can	how	one	their	who
did	into	only	them	with
do	is	or	they	work
down	it	other	this	world
each	make	out	time	you
even	many	over	to	

Content Words

ball	goal	kick	run	uniforms
best	goalie(s)	knees	score	wear
cleats	grass	legs	scoreboard	winning
everyone	guards	net	shin	worth
feet	hands	play(ed, er, ers)	soccer	
field	heads	point(s)	sport	
follow	hit	referees	team(s, 's)	
game	keep	rules	tries	

··· About the Author

Mary Lindeen is a writer, editor, parent, and former elementary school teacher. She has written more than 100 books for children and edited many more. She specializes in early literacy instruction and books for young readers, especially nonfiction.

··· About the Advisor

Dr. Shannon Cannon is a teacher educator in the School of Education at UC Davis, where she also earned her Ph.D. in Language, Literacy, and Culture. She serves on the clinical faculty, supervising pre-service teachers and teaching elementary methods courses in reading, effective teaching, and teacher action research.